SPORTS CARS

by
Sean McCollum

Consultants:

Jeffrey Dahnert, President, CEO
Michael Lewis, Director
Sports Car Club of America
Topeka, Kansas

CAPSTONE PRESS
a capstone imprint

Edge Books are published by Capstone Press,
151 Good Counsel Drive, P.O. Box 669, Mankato, Minnesota 56002.
www.capstonepress.com

092009
005619WZS10

 Books published by Capstone Press are manufactured with paper
containing at least 10 percent post-consumer waste.

Library of Congress Cataloging-in-Publication Data
McCollum, Sean.
    Sports cars / by Sean McCollum.
    p. cm. — (Edge books. Full throttle)
    Summary: "Describes the history, parts, and performance of sports cars" — Provided
by publisher.
    Includes bibliographical references and index.
    ISBN 978-1-4296-3944-6 (lib. bdg.)
    1. Sports cars — Juvenile literature. I. Title. II. Series.
TL236.M37285 2010
629.222'1 — dc22   2009028639

Editorial Credits
Abby Czeskleba, editor; Tracy Davies, designer; Jo Miller, media researcher;
    Laura Manthe, production specialist

Photo Credits
AP Images/Steve Nesius, 27
Getty Images for Grand Am/Brian Cleary, cover, 17
Getty Images Inc./AFP/Jean Francois Monier, 5; Marcel Mochet, 7, 23; Darrell Ingham, 21;
    Fox Photos, 12; Klemantaski Collection, 14; RacingOne, 15; Rick Dole, 9, 18, 25, 28;
    Roger Viollet/Branger, 11; Streeter Lecka, 22, 29;
Shutterstock/Max Earey, 19, 20

Artistic Effects
Dreamstime/In-finity; Dreamstime/Michaelkovachev; iStockphoto/Michael Irwin;
iStockphoto/Russell Tate; Shutterstock/Els Jooren; Shutterstock/Fedorov Oleksiy;
Shutterstock/jgl247; Shutterstock/Marilyn Volan; Shutterstock/Pocike

Capstone Press thanks Scott Atherton of ALMS.

Table of Contents

A DAY OF RACING

The Audi No. 2 could not keep up with the Peugeot No. 7 at the 2008 24 Hours of Le Mans. These Le Mans **Prototypes** had been two of the favorites to win the event. But now the race was half over and the Peugeot had a two-minute lead. Both cars were averaging more than 130 miles (209 kilometers) per hour.

When the rain started, the Audi No. 2 switched to grooved tires during a pit stop. The new tires got better grip on the slick track. The Audi proved faster than the Peugeot in the wet conditions. The Audi took the lead in the 13th hour of the race.

In the end, the Audi's three drivers lifted the huge trophy over their heads. They had just won the top sports car race in the world. It was the Audi team's fifth-straight win at the 24 Hours of Le Mans.

The Audi team completed a record 381 laps around the 8.5-mile (13.7-kilometer) track. That equaled more than 3,000 miles (4,828 kilometers).

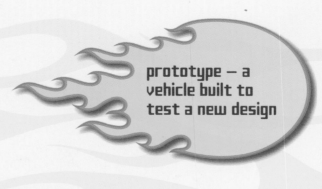

prototype — a vehicle built to test a new design

The Audi No. 2 (left) and Peugeot No. 7 (right) raced for the title at the 2008 24 Hours of Le Mans.

Fast Fact: At races like the 24 Hours of Le Mans, two to three drivers make up one team. They trade places every one to two hours. Switching places keeps drivers from getting tired.

SPORTS CAR RACING

Sports car races are different from other motorsports races. Stock cars and open-wheel racers like Indy cars compete to see who can complete a set number of laps in the shortest time. Most stock car races cover 500 miles (805 kilometers) or less. But many sports car races are **endurance races** like the 24 Hours of Le Mans. These races measure how far cars can travel in a set time or how fast they can travel a set distance. Common distances are 620 miles (998 kilometers) and 1,000 miles (1,609 kilometers). Many endurance races last 12 or 24 hours.

Endurance races test a car's durability and reliability. Some races keep cars rolling day and night. The long-distance challenge takes its toll. The engineering and endurance needed to succeed make sports car racing one of the most difficult competitions in motorsports.

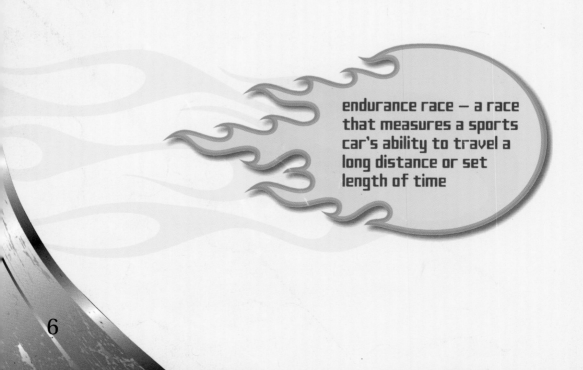

endurance race — a race that measures a sports car's ability to travel a long distance or set length of time

Many people consider the 24 Hours of Le Mans to be one of the greatest long-distance races in motorsports.

Fast Fact: Oftentimes fewer than half the cars finish the 24 Hours of Le Mans.

FOUR RACES WITHIN A RACE

People who have never seen a sports car race may scratch their heads after watching an event. The **cockpits** of some cars are open while others have windshields. Certain styles of cars are clearly faster than others. The fastest cars like the Audi R10 and Peugeot 908 look like machines of the future. Others, like the Porsche 911 and Dodge Viper GTS-R, look like the sports cars that cruise the highways.

There are two main categories of cars in sports car racing: Le Mans Prototypes (LMPs) and Grand Touring (GT) cars. Each category is divided into two classes. Le Mans Prototypes are divided into the LMP1 and LMP2 classes. Grand Touring cars are divided into GT1 and GT2 classes. The four classes have different rules for speed and engine size. A winner is crowned in each class at the end of every race.

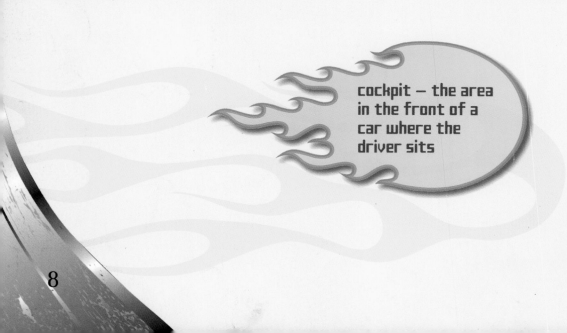

cockpit — the area in the front of a car where the driver sits

8

The Peugeot 908 (top) has a closed cockpit while the Audi R10 (bottom) has an open cockpit.

Fast Fact: All competition sports cars must have two seats even though the passenger's seat is not used.

About 100 years ago, Grand Prix was the most popular form of car racing in Europe. These races showed off the power and speed of early race cars. At the same time, racing teams began endurance racing. The first 24-hour race took place at Brooklands racetrack in 1907 near London, England. The 24 Hours of Le Mans was first run in 1923 in Le Mans, France. It remains the world's most famous endurance race because of its great racing history.

The challenge of endurance racing pushed carmakers to build better cars. Endurance races became a proving ground for engines, **chassis**, transmissions, suspension systems, and brakes. If a part proved itself in such tough racing conditions, carmakers soon built it into regular road cars.

Cars didn't change much during the 1930s. But after World War II (1939–1945), the needs of Grand Prix and endurance racing gave rise to different designs. Grand Prix race cars gradually turned into Formula 1 (F1) open-wheel race cars. Sports cars kept their wheels covered. They were built to travel longer distances than Grand Prix race cars.

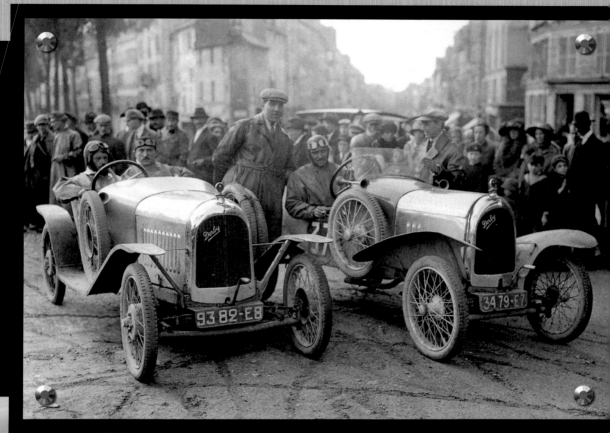

Large crowds gathered to watch people race during the early 1920s.

chassis — the frame on which the body of a vehicle is built

Disaster of 1955

Mercedes-Benz had high hopes for its 300SLR sports car in the 1955 24 Hours of Le Mans. But early in the race, driver Pierre Levegh hit the back of another car at more than 150 miles (241 kilometers) per hour. His car flew into a barrier and ripped apart in a fireball. Its engine, flaming chassis, and other parts tore through the crowd. More than 75 people were killed, including Levegh.

The 1955 crash remains the deadliest disaster in racing history. It led to changes in track design to better protect drivers and fans. Today, racing fans stand farther away from the track than they once did.

Levegh's car exploded after crashing into a barrier.

Winning a big race like Le Mans was great for carmakers. Championship cars helped companies like Audi, Acura, and Porsche sell more road-going production vehicles. These companies poured money into racing teams to test new technologies, win races, and impress new customers.

Sports car prototypes changed the look and speed of sports car racing after 1953. These race cars were small, light, and their engines lacked a great deal of **horsepower**. To make up for the lack of power, designers built chassis that helped the cars cut through the air. But these **aerodynamic** improvements created problems. The cars sometimes lifted off the track at high speeds. The cars became dangerous and difficult to handle during races.

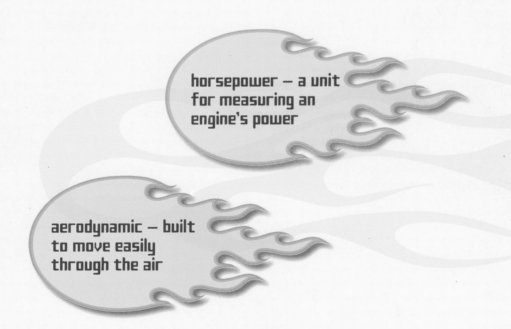

horsepower – a unit for measuring an engine's power

aerodynamic – built to move easily through the air

13

DOWNFORCE MAKES THE DIFFERENCE

In the 1950s, Swiss engineer Michael May thought of a solution. He attached an upside-down wing to his Porsche Type 550. The wing created **downforce**. Instead of lifting up, this wing pushed the car down onto the track. The wings gave drivers better control.

May's downforce idea took a while to catch on. In 1966, American Jim Hall added a wing to the back of his 2E Can-Am Chaparral. The wing looked like a big table mounted on the back of his sports car prototype. But the wing clearly improved the car's handling. The wing idea finally caught on among sports car, F1, and Indy car designers.

The rear wing improved a car's traction, grip, and handling.

downforce – the force of passing air pressing down on a moving vehicle

Car designers continued to experiment with sports car prototypes. Since 1994, both LMP1s and LMP2s have gone through rule changes for engine size, chassis design, and other features.

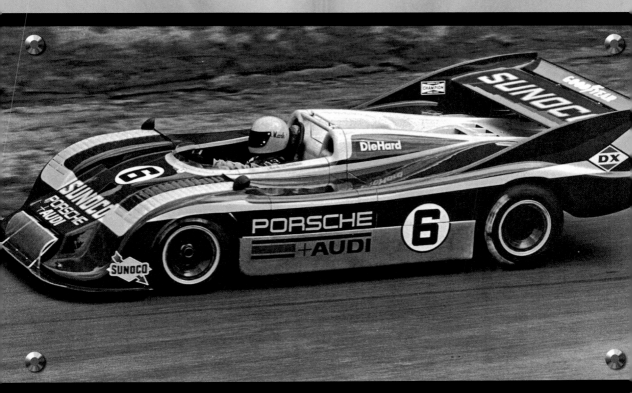

Mark Donohue was the only person to drive the Porsche 917-30. The car produced more than 1,200 horsepower.

Fast Fact: Mark Donohue lost only one race with the Porsche 917-30 during the 1973 Can-Am Series.

3 TODAY'S SPORTS CARS

The lineup in today's sports cars races includes Daytona Prototypes, Le Mans Prototypes (LMPs), and Grand Touring (GT) cars. The engineering and speed of these cars make them wonders of the racing world.

DAYTONA PROTOTYPES

Daytona Prototypes are the heavier, less expensive cousins of the LMPs. Daytona Prototypes are built for the racetrack. In the United States, Daytona Prototypes race in the Rolex Sports Car Series.

While each car's chassis is specially designed, manufacturers can make very few **modifications**. Rules require Daytona Prototypes to weigh at least 2,225 pounds (1,009 kilograms). These cars produce 500 horsepower and reach speeds of 195 miles (314 kilometers) per hour.

modification – a change made to the chassis or other part of a car

The No. 99 Pontiac takes the lead at a
2007 Grand Am Rolex Sports Car Series race.

Fast Fact: The chassis of a
Daytona Prototype can cost
more than $500,000.

LMP1s are one-of-a-kind racing machines with custom engines. The cars must weigh at least 1,985 pounds (900 kilograms). Car companies like Porsche and Audi usually sponsor LMP1 teams.

LMP1s are powered by the biggest engines in sports car racing. LMP1 engines may have 10 or 12 cylinders. However, there is no limit to the number of cylinders in this class. The cars do have a limit of 700 horsepower. Even with horsepower limits, LMP1s accelerate from 0 to 100 miles (161 kilometers) per hour in three seconds. The cars can reach more than 200 miles (322 kilometers) per hour.

Audi R15 TDI

Top LMP1 models include the Audi R10 TDI and the Audi R15 TDI. While these models may look similar, they are different under the hood. The R10 TDI's engine has 12 cylinders while the R15 TDI's engine has 10.

The chassis of LMP1s have a carbon-fiber shell over a honeycombed core of aluminum. This combination is lightweight but strong. The design helps protect drivers in crashes.

Audi R10 TDI

LMP1s and LMP2s have the same chassis, but there are differences between the two classes. For starters, LMP2s are smaller and weigh at least 165 pounds (75 kilograms) less than LMP1s. LMP2s also use smaller engines that produce up to 550 horsepower. But LMP2s have outraced LMP1s even though LMP2s have less powerful engines. Models of LMP2s include the Porsche RS Spyder, Acura ARX-01b, and Lola B09/80. LMP1s and LMP2s can have either an open or closed canopy. Cars with closed canopies must have a windshield, roof, and two doors.

Overall, LMP2s are less expensive to build and race. The lower cost makes it easier for private owners, called privateers, to compete in the LMP2 class.

Porsche RS Spyder

GRAND TOURING 1

Grand Touring (GT) cars aren't as high-tech or as fast as the sports prototypes. But they still are plenty quick. Both GT1s and GT2s can reach speeds of 180 miles (290 kilometers) or more during a race.

Cars in the Grand Touring 1 (GT1) class look like factory-made sports cars. But GT1s can be changed for racing. Teams can improve aerodynamics, install bigger brakes, and add wider tires. GT1 engines can produce a maximum of 650 horsepower. They must weigh at least 2,535 pounds (1,150 kilograms). Top competition models of GT1s include the Aston Martin DBR9, Corvette C6.R, and Saleen S7R.

Corvette C6.R

GRAND TOURING 2

GT2s cannot be changed as much as GT1s. GT2s must weigh at least 2,480 pounds (1,125 kilograms). Their engines have a limit of 500 horsepower. They are similar to street sports cars. But GT2s also have added safety features like **roll cages**. Top competition models of GT2s include the Ferrari F430 GT, Dodge Viper Competition Coupe, and Ford GT-R.

Dodge Viper Competition Coupe

roll cage – a structure of strong metal tubing in a sports car that surrounds and protects the driver

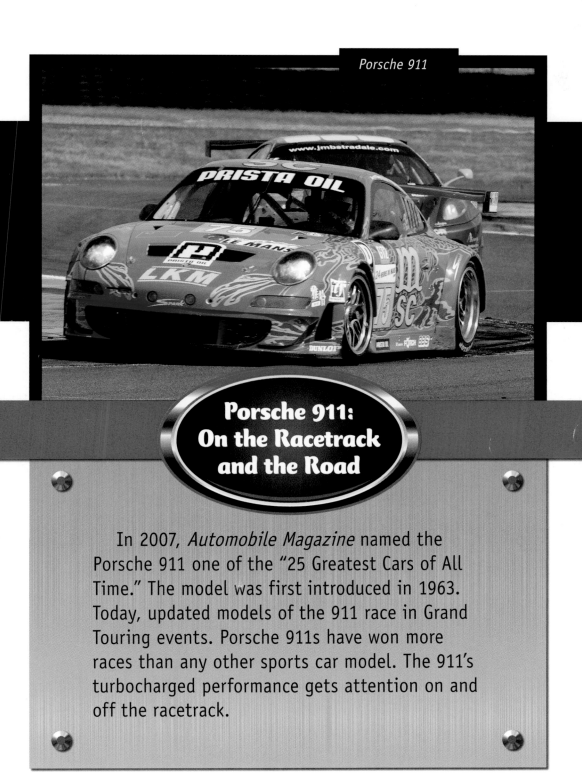

Porsche 911: On the Racetrack and the Road

In 2007, *Automobile Magazine* named the Porsche 911 one of the "25 Greatest Cars of All Time." The model was first introduced in 1963. Today, updated models of the 911 race in Grand Touring events. Porsche 911s have won more races than any other sports car model. The 911's turbocharged performance gets attention on and off the racetrack.

Racing fans love to watch their favorite drivers zoom around the track. Road courses provide all-around tests for the different classes of cars. Straight stretches call for power and speed, but the courses also feature **chicanes**. These layouts test a car's handling, braking, and acceleration.

SPORTS CAR SERIES AND RACES

Major sports car races take place all over the world. Most are included in a series, where teams rack up points for top finishes. The standings add excitement as cars and drivers fight for the championship in their class.

The Le Mans Series (LMS) consists of four to six races. Most of these races are held in Europe. The Nürburgring race in Germany is 621 miles (1,000 kilometers) long. Europe also hosts the FIA GT3 European Championship and the World Touring Car Championship.

In the United States, drivers compete in the American Le Mans Series.

chicane —a tight turn that forces cars to slow down on a racetrack

AMERICAN LE MANS SERIES

In the United States, sports car racing has gained popularity thanks to the American Le Mans Series (ALMS). Started in 1999, this series borrows its name from the French race. Cars racing in the ALMS feature three "leader lights." These lights on the side of the cars help fans follow the race. The 1st place car displays one light, 2nd place shows two lights, and 3rd place shows three lights. The lights in each class are different colors.

The ALMS hosts 10 races in North America every year, including the 12 Hours of Sebring at Florida's Sebring International Raceway. Racing teams view this track as a good tune up for 24 Hours of Le Mans in June. Racing legends Mario Andretti, Jim Hall, and A. J. Foyt have all won at Sebring International Raceway.

In October, the Petit Le Mans is held at the Road Atlanta road course in Georgia. The race's name means "small Le Mans" in French. This race runs for 1,000 miles (1,609 kilometers) or 10 hours, whichever comes first.

The 12 Hours of Sebring is one of the races in the American Le Mans Series.

Fast Fact: Sebring International Raceway is the oldest road course in North America.

In the Pits

During endurance races, LMPs head for the pits about once every hour. GTs can go a little longer before needing to stop. Racing teams must follow rules for refueling and tire changes. Here's what happens during a regular pit stop:

1. The car pulls into the pit box. The driver turns off the engine. Switching off the engine makes refueling safe.
2. Five pit crew members jump over the pit wall to work on the car. First, they fuel the car.
3. Once fueling is finished, the pit crew replaces all four tires in six to 10 seconds.
4. The driver starts the car and roars back onto the course.

Pit stops during endurance races may take much longer. To fix big problems, the team may roll the car into the garage for as long as 30 minutes.

The team can switch drivers during refueling, but no other work can be done.

ROLEX SPORTS CAR SERIES

The Rolex Sports Car Series includes the Rolex 24 held at Daytona International Speedway. Daytona Prototypes rule this endurance race. The Rolex Sports Car Series also features 10 shorter races of 200 or 250 miles (322 or 402 kilometers).

Racing teams work year-round to create top sports cars. As sports car designs improve, road-going production sports cars will become tougher and safer.

Fast Fact: The closest finish in the history of 24-hour endurance races happened at the 2009 Rolex Sports Car Series. The first two drivers finished within .167 second of each other.

GLOSSARY

aerodynamic (air-oh-dye-NA-mik) — built to move easily through the air

chassis (CHA-see) — the main framework of a vehicle to which the other parts are fixed

chicane (shih-KANE) — a tight turn that forces cars to slow down on a racetrack

cockpit (KOK-pit) — the area of a sports car where the driver sits

cylinder (SI-luhn-duhr) — one of the hollow cylindrical-shaped chambers inside an engine; fuel burns in the cylinders to create power.

downforce (DOUN-fors) — the downward air pressure that helps a race car grip the track

endurance race (en-DUR-enss RAYSS) — a race that measures a sports car's ability to travel a long distance or set length of time

handling (HAND-ling) — how well a car steers and operates on the road

horsepower (HORSS-pou-ur) — a unit for measuring an engine's power

modification (mod-uh-fi-KAY-shuhn) — a change made to the chassis or other part of a car

prototype (PROH-tow-tipe) — a vehicle built to test a new design

roll cage (ROHL KAYJ) — a structure of strong metal tubing in a sports car that surrounds and protects the driver

turbocharger (TUR-boh-char-juhr) — a system that forces air through an engine to make a car go faster

READ MORE

Doeden, Matt. *Sports Car Racing*. Motor Mania. Minneapolis: Lerner, 2009.

Graham, Ian. *Fast Cars*. How Machines Work. Mankato, Minn.: Black Rabbit Books, 2009.

Woods, Bob. *Hottest Sports Cars*. Wild Wheels! Berkeley Heights, N.J.: Enslow, 2008.

INTERNET SITES

FactHound offers a safe, fun way to find Internet sites related to this book. All of the sites on FactHound have been researched by our staff.

Here's all you do:

Visit *www.facthound.com*

FactHound will fetch the best sites for you!

Index